D0915564

The Perfect Brew

A presentation of coffees and teas

Cover Photo ©1995 Superstock, Inc.

Compiled by Deborah Hansen

Cover Design by Todd Kelsey

Published by
Great Quotations Publishing Co.,
Glendale Heights, IL

ISBN 1-56245-213-4

Printed in Hong Kong

Table of Contents:

THE HISTORY
OF COFFEE

The very early history of coffee is very sketchy, but we do know that coffee was prepared the way we know it by the late sixteenth century. There have been many writings describing an Arab "snooty syrup" made from "burnt" seeds.

It was several more years before Europeans discovered the drink.

When coffee finally made its European debut, it was introduced as a medicine. It was used for curing a great variety of illnesses. The Europeans only later learned that the Arab nations drank coffee because they liked its flavor rather than using it as a medicine.

By the time Europeans developed a taste for coffee, the Arabs had already established a monopoly on the coffee-bean trade. They closely guarded "their" bean.

They would roast them before being shipped to Europe, and all visitors were forbidden to visit coffee plantations, afraid that a stray bean or cutting may leave the country with them.

Inevitably, with so many pilgrims trampling the fields on their way to Mecca, some of the beans escaped. The first live coffee plant was brought to Europe in 1616, smuggled in by the Dutch. Over the next seventy years, as the Dutch cultivated the bean in large plantations all over Indonesia, thus coffee became the favorite beverage of the Netherlands.

It took several decades of avid coffee consumption for the drink to reach the domestic circle, but when it did, it remained a social beverage. Coffee was not enjoyed alone; it was offered to honored guests as a sign of hospitality, and it was an outrage not to drink coffee with one's host (and an even greater outrage for a host not to offer it!)

Today, the United States drinks nearly 47 million cups of coffee a day. Until recently, coffee was mostly drank in the home or office. Now we see many coffee shops opening, offering a wide variety of this roasted bean we call, coffee.

How Coffee
IS ROASTED

There are three roasting stages that the beans pass through as they progress from green beans to the rich brown coffee beans we find at the store. In the first stage, the roastmaster applies heat to bring the water in the beans close to the boiling point, which drives off all free moisture in the beans.

In the second stage, heat, air flow and roasting time are carefully controlled by the roastmaster to bring the internal temperature of the beans to between 320° and 480° degrees F (depending on the bean type and roast desired).

During this stage, the cell walls of the coffee beans are broken down and the coffee's complex polysacharides within are converted to starches and sugars.

The natural sugars of the bean also caramelize, which results in the characteristically rich brown color of the roasted beans. In this breakdown process, substances called aromatics are formed along with oils, fats, waxes and carbohydrates which add to the flavor complexity in the final brewed cup of coffee. The oils, fats and carbohydrates provide body and help suspend and contain the many delicate and volatile aromatics within the cup.

As the roast continues, additional complex substances are broken down into simpler components and the many volatile oils are driven outward toward the beans surface. This is considered the third stage and is characterized by an oily appearance on the outside of the bean. Full city roast is a term used to describe this approximate stage.

It is the darkest roast achievable before the volatile oils are driven off by further application of heat. Going beyond this point, such as for French or Italian roasts, drives some of the aromatics completely from the beans (as well as some of the unique and distinguishing flavors). For these types of roasts, the roastmaster chooses to trade off those distinguishing varietal flavors in favor of the French roast taste that some people prefer.

MAKING A GOOD POT
OF COFFEE

1. Start with good quality beans.
2. Use clean equipment.
3. Use fresh water.
4. Use the correct grind for your particular machine.
5. Use the right amount of coffee.
6. Serve coffee fresh.

Starting with good beans is very important. Don't expect a great cup of coffee from old beans or a cheaper brand of bean.

Use equipment that is very clean. Coffee tends to leave a residue on pots and filters and should be washed out with baking soda and a scrub brush. Don't use dish soap. It tends to leave a residue behind.

Consider drinking coffee as if you were drinking water (your coffee is 98% water). If you drink your water directly from the tap, use it.

But if you water has a lot of minerals or other substances in it, then consider a water filter or bottled water. Make sure the water is cool.

If coffee brewing is done properly, the brewed pot should contain between 18 and 22 percent of the ground coffee weight in extracted solubles. If it contains less, the coffee will taste bland and watery; if it contains a higher percentage, the brew will taste harsh and bitter.

The amount of extraction is determined by the fineness of the coffee grind and the length of time that the hot water is in contact with the coffee grounds.

The amount of coffee you should use for a full-bodied and flavorful cup of coffee is 2 level tablespoons per 6-ounce cup. Some people try to stretch the grind and put in a little less of a finer grind but they will wind up with a thin, bitter coffee. Don't ruin your coffee at this final stage since you've gotten this far!

Finally, serve coffee within 20 minutes after brewing. The aromatics start to evaporate immediately after brewing and the coffee suffers a loss of flavor. To keep coffee's flavor after 20 minutes, store in a vacuum thermos to retain its freshness.

COFFEE DRINK
RECIPES

For all the following
combinations start with:

6oz. Freshly brewed hot coffee

Kona Nut
1 oz. Kahlua
1 oz. Frangelico

Irish Eyes
1 oz. Irish whiskey
1 oz. Bailey's Irish Cream

Alexander

1 oz. creme de cacao
1 oz. brandy

Mocha

1 oz. Kahlua
1 oz. creme de cacao

Amore

1 oz. amaretto
1 oz. brandy

Brown Velvet

1 oz. Triple Sec
1 oz. creme de cacao

Moose milk

1 1/2 quarts milk
1 quart half and half
1 cup creme de cacao
1 cup Kahlua
1 fifth dark rum
1/2 gallon ice cream
nutmeg

In large bowl, mix all ingredients except ice cream and nutmeg. Scoop ice cream into mixture. Pour into cups and dust with nutmeg. Serves 10-12.

Hot Kisses

6 oz. freshly brewed coffee
1 oz. Kahlua
1 oz. creme de banana
whipped cream
nutmeg

Mix above ingredients except
cream and nutmeg. Top with
whipping cream and nutmeg
Makes single serving.

COFFEE DESSERTS

Coffee Nut Kisses

1 3/4 cups toasted almonds
1/4 cup whole coffee beans
1 1/2 cups sugar
2 egg whites
1 teaspoon vanilla extract
Mocha beans (optional)

Heat oven to 325°F. Lightly grease two baking sheets. Finely grind the almonds and coffee beans with half of the sugar. Add the egg whites and process until well combined. Add the rest of the sugar and the vanilla extract and blend well.

Shape the dough into 1-inch balls, and place them about 1/2 inch apart on the prepared baking sheets. Top with mocha beans, if desired. Bake until firm and lightly colored, about 20 minutes.
Makes about 40 cookies.

Moist Mocha Cake

10 ounces bittersweet chocolate,
broken into pieces
3/4 cup butter
1 cup sugar
3 tablespoons instant coffee
granules
5 egg yolks
1/3 cup cake flour
5 egg whites
Confectioner's sugar for dusting

Heat oven to 350°F. Butter a 9-inch cake pan. Combine chocolate, butter and sugar in the top of a double boiler over simmering water and stir until chocolate melts. Mix in the instant coffee and let cool. Whisk the egg yolks into the chocolate mixture.

Whisk in the flour.

Beat the egg whites just until they form stiff peaks, be careful not to overbeat.

Add one-third of the egg whites to the chocolate mixture and mix well. Carefully fold in the remaining whites, mixing only until they are incorporated and no streaks of white are visible in the batter. Do not overmix.

Pour the batter into the prepared pan and bake until the cake is firm to the touch, 35 to 40 minutes. Cool thoroughly on a rack. Dust with the confectioner's sugar, if desired.

Mocha Chip Cookies

1 1/4 cups butter at room
temperature
1 cup confectioner's sugar
1/2 cup brown sugar
1/4 teaspoon salt
2 tablespoons instant coffee
powder
1 tablespoon hot water
1/2 teaspoon coffee extract
2 1/2 cups all-purpose flour
2 teaspoons baking powder
2 cups chocolate chips
1/2 cup granulated sugar for
rolling the cookies in

Heat over to 350°F. Lightly grease several baking sheets. Cream the butter, confectioner's sugar, brown sugar and salt with an electric mixer until very creamy (about 2 minutes.) Dissolve the instant coffee in the hot water, and stir into the butter mixture. Add the coffee extract and beat well.

Sift together the flour and baking powder, and gradually add the dry ingredients to the batter, stirring just until incorporated. Fold in the chocolate chips.

Shape dough into 1-inch balls, rolling in the granulated sugar, and place 1 inch apart on prepared baking sheets. Bake for about 15 minutes, until they are a pale golden brown.

Makes 60 cookies.

Toffee Ice Cream Torte

1 cup almond macaroon crumbs
2 tbs. melted butter
1 quart chocolate ice cream,
slightly softened
1 cup fudge sauce
1 quart coffee ice cream, slightly
softened
4 Heath toffee bars, coarsely
chopped

Combine crumbs and butter and
press on bottom of a 9-inch
springform pan. Bake at 350° for
8 to 10 minutes or until golden.

Cool. Spread chocolate ice cream evenly on crust, drizzle with chocolate sauce and freeze until firm. Spread with coffee ice cream and sprinkle with chopped toffee.

Drizzle with remaining fudge sauce. Cover and freeze until firm.

To serve, remove from freezer several minutes before slicing. Cut into wedges with a hot, wet knife.

Coffee Caramels

1 cup heavy cream
1 1/4 cups sugar
pinch salt
1/2 cup very mild honey
1 teaspoon coffee extract
1 tablespoon unsalted butter

Butter a 9x5 inch loaf pan and
place by the stove.
In a small, heavy saucepan, heat
the cream until it boils.
Stir in the sugar, salt, and honey.
Bring the mixture back to a boil
and cook, stirring occasionally ,
for about 10 minutes or until a
candy thermometer reads 257°F.

Remove the pan from the heat and stir in the coffee extract and the butter. Pour the candy into the loaf pan and let it cool completely. If the caramel feels too soft after it has cooled, scrape it back into the saucepan and boil it for another 2 minutes. It should be firmer now.

With a buttered knife, cut the caramel into squares, re-buttering the knife as necessary. Wrap the squares in plastic or wax paper, and store them in an airtight container in the refrigerator for up to two weeks.

Makes about 1 pound.

Mocha Chocolate Chip Cheesecake

Crust:
6 tbs. butter, melted
1 1/2 cups chocolate wafer
crumbs
2 tbs. sugar

Combine crust ingredients and
press into bottom and partially
up sides of a buttered 10-inch
spingform pan. Bake at 350° for
10 minutes. Cool while making
filling. Turn oven temperature
to 200°.

Filling:

1 1/2 lb. cream cheese, room
temperature
1 cup sugar
4 eggs, room temperature
1/3 cup heavy cream
1 tbs. instant coffee powder
1 tsp. vanilla
6 oz. mini semisweet chocolate
chips

Using the steel knife of a food processor, combine cream cheese and sugar until light. Add the eggs and process until smooth, scrape down the sides of the bowl. Add the instant coffee and vanilla and combine. Pour half of the filling into the prepared crust. Stir the chocolate chips into the remaining filling an carefully pour over the filling in the pan. Bake for 2 hours until set. Cool at room temperature. Cover with plastic wrap and refrigerate overnight.

Mocha Chip Muffins

1/2 cup butter
1/2 cup brown sugar
1/2 cup granulated sugar
2 tbs instant coffee
2 tsp. vanilla
2 eggs
2/3 cup milk
1 3/4 cup flour
1/2 tsp. salt
1 tbsp. baking powder
1 cup semisweet chocolate chips
1 cup chopped walnuts

Preheat over to 350°. Cream butter, sugars, coffee and vanilla until light and fluffy. Beat together eggs and milk. Sift together flour, salt and baking powder. Add wet ingredients and dry ingredients to butter mixture, stirring just to combine. Add chips and nuts. Line twelve 3-inch muffin cups with paper liners or grease and flour well. Divide batter evenly into muffin tins. Bake for 20-25 minutes.

COFFEE TRIVIA

• Coffee may be frozen for up to 3 months without losing quality.

• The average cup of coffee contains 100 milligrams of caffeine.

• The average cup of espresso contains 80 milligrams of caffeine.

• Green coffee beans keep indefinitely.

• The average American adult consumes 26.7 gallons of coffee per year.

• In Turkey and Greece it is customary for the oldest person present to be served their coffee first.

• Arabica beans account for 90% of the world's coffee output.

• The most popular beverages in the world are:
    1) water
    2) tea
    3) coffee.

- The average American adult consumes 10.2 pounds of coffee beans per year.

- The United States consumes over 20% of the world's coffee.

- Tea contains half as much caffeine as coffee.

- Each coffee tree produces about 2,000 beans per year.

TEA
HISTORY OF TEA

Legend has it that Chinese Emperor Shen Nung was always drinking boiled water, convinced that this would protect him from the prevalent diseases of the time.

One day, while his servants were boiling his water, a few leaves from a nearby camellia bush caught a breeze and floated down into the heating water. The emperor's attention was caught by the aroma which arose from the pot.

Fascinated by the aroma, he drank some of the stock. He was immediately infatuated by the taste and quality of the brew, and knew he had discovered something of wondrous importance.

News of the emperor's discovery spread quickly throughout China, and soon everyone was trying the beverage. Before long tea became an important part of Chinese culture. As the centuries passed and trade with the West opened up, the status of tea increased.

In America, tea was the beverage of choice until the Revolution. When the British passed the Tea Act of 1773, the Colonists boycotted tea completely. A group of Colonists, dressed as American Indians, threw the tea from three ships into the harbor in what is known as the Boston Tea Party.

After the Revolution, tea became popular again, and the trade between China and America flourished.

Great fortunes were made as ships from the Atlantic ports sailed around Cape Horn to the Pacific Northwest. They loaded their ships with furs to trade in the orient for tea, silk and spices.

Iced tea and the teabag are recent American inventions. Iced tea was first served at the World's Fair in St. Louis in 1901. It was a very hot steamy day and an enterprising tea salesman poured tea over ice, and the crowds loved it. We've been drinking iced tea ever since, and today over 80% of the domestic tea market in the U.S. is served as iced tea.

In New York in 1908 another enterprising tea salesman began sending his samples to retailers in small silk bags. Assuming the tea was to be steeped in the bags, the retailers put them right into their pots. They loved the convenience of the premeasured, self-straining bags and ordered more!

Today, Americans use over 200 million pounds of tea per year. Most of it comes from China, India and Sri Lanka. The United Kingdom imports almost twice that amount.

Tea Types

<u>The Tea Plant</u>
Tea comes from a plant called
Camellia Sinensis, a bushy
member of the evergreen family,
it grows in tropical or
subtropical climates. A climate
with 50 inches of annual rainfall
is ideal for growing tea.

Much like grapes (used to make wine) which take on a certain characteristic of soil and climate, the tea plant also takes on a distinct flavor from the climate and soil in which it is grown. If left unpruned, a tea plant will grow to a height of over 50 feet. Most plants are pruned, trained and clipped to a flat surface for ease in picking and are about four feet tall. A tea plant may remain productive for over a century. There are three categories of Tea: Black, Green and Oolong.

Black Tea

Black teas undergo two processes. First leaves are placed on racks and dried out so that they lose about half of their moisture content. Then they are exposed to very hot air. This heat turns the leaves black. After the leaves cool, they are shipped to destinations where they will be sold either as a single leaf or as a blend. Black teas are the ones that produce the hearty brews to which we Westerners have become accustomed.

Types of Black Teas

Darjeeling

This tea is grown at high altitudes and is famous for its fragrance and wine-like taste. This is called the Champagne of teas. It is a very expensive tea and is used in many blends.

Ceylon

This tea is grown at high altitude, and produces a rich, golden brew. This tea is used in many blends and is also very tasty on its own any time of day.

Earl Gray

This tea is a combination of Darjeeling and China Black that has been scented with oil of Bergamot (and Italian citrus fruit.) It is exotic in both aroma and taste.

English Breakfast

This tea is a blend of Ceylon and a variety of Indian teas. This tea produces a strong, full-bodied brew that is a favorite for breakfast, but is good throughout the day.

Green Teas

Green teas are a non-fermented tea. These leaves are steamed in large vats rather than exposed to hot air. Green teas have a very delicate flavor, and when brewed have a very light color. They are naturally low in caffeine and can be very soothing, (the most popular is Jasmine.) They are best enjoyed plain and are said to settle upset stomachs.

Oolong Teas

Oolong teas are a compromise between black and green teas. They are partially fermented and are more delicate than black tea but stronger than green tea. Oolongs also have a lower caffeine content than black teas.

BREWING TEA

A Pot of Tea

To brew a pot of tea, first fill a kettle with cold water and bring it to a rolling boil. Only use fresh cold water; it has more oxygen and makes a better brew. Preheat a separate teapot by rinsing with very hot tap water. Use 1 teabag for each desired cup of tea. Once the water has boiled, bring the teapot to the kettle and pour in the appropriate amount of water.

Cover with the lid and let the tea steep for 3-5 minutes. (Tea releases its color long before its flavor, so its color is no indication of the proper strength.)

Just before pouring, stir the tea to evenly distribute the flavor. Any tea left in the pot for longer than 10 minutes will develop an off flavor if the leaves are not removed. Milk is generally used with black tea, but never in green or oolong. Milk neutralizes the tannins in the tea and reduces the astringency. Some like lemon, sugar, or honey in their tea, but it is simply a matter of taste.

A Cup of Tea

To brew a cup of tea, fill a kettle with cold water and bring to a boil. Place a tea bag or a teaspoon of loose tea encased in a tea ball or spoon. Fill the cup with boiling water, leaving room for milk if you wish. Let the tea brew 3 to 5 minutes. Remove the bag (give it a good squeeze) the ball, and serve.

Tea Recipes

Brown Sugar Cookies

1 cup dark brown sugar
1/2 cup unsalted butter
1 egg
2 cups flour
1 teaspoon milk
1/4 cup sugar

Preheat oven to 350°.
Cream together the brown sugar
and butter. Add the egg and
beat until the mixture is light
and fluffy. Stir in the flour and
baking soda, making sure all the
ingredients are thoroughly
incorporated. Beat in the milk.

On a floured surface, roll the dough out to 1/4-inch thickness. Using a 2 1/2-inch biscuit or cookie cutter, cut out the cookies and place them on an ungreased cookie sheet. Sprinkle each cookie lightly with sugar. Bake 10 to 12 minutes, or until bottoms and edges are lightly browned. Cool on a rack. Makes 3 dozen.

Stuffed Strawberries

2 to 3 dozen very red strawberries
8 oz. cream cheese, softened
1/2 cup powdered Grand Mariner or orange juice
1 orange rind grated

Remove green tops from strawberries. Cut pointed end into wedges like a pie, cutting about 2/3 of the way down. If the berrys are small, make two cuts; if large, make three cuts, dividing the berry into 6 wedges.

Combine cream cheese, sugar, Grand Mariner, and zest using a mixer until well blended. Place in pastry bag fitted with a fluted tip. Pipe mixture into center of each berry. Garnish with mint leaves or flower if desired. Can be stored in the refrigerator for several hours.

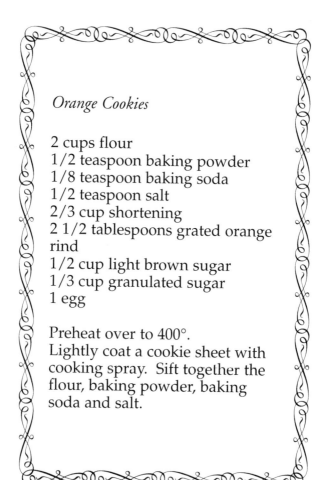

Orange Cookies

2 cups flour
1/2 teaspoon baking powder
1/8 teaspoon baking soda
1/2 teaspoon salt
2/3 cup shortening
2 1/2 tablespoons grated orange rind
1/2 cup light brown sugar
1/3 cup granulated sugar
1 egg

Preheat over to 400°.
Lightly coat a cookie sheet with cooking spray. Sift together the flour, baking powder, baking soda and salt.

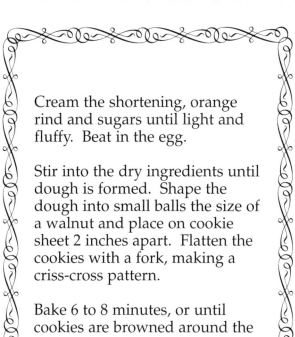

Cream the shortening, orange rind and sugars until light and fluffy. Beat in the egg.

Stir into the dry ingredients until dough is formed. Shape the dough into small balls the size of a walnut and place on cookie sheet 2 inches apart. Flatten the cookies with a fork, making a criss-cross pattern.

Bake 6 to 8 minutes, or until cookies are browned around the edges. Cool on a rack.

Makes 2 1/2 to 3 dozen cookies.

Cheese and Date Pastries

1 cup butter
8 oz. sharp cheddar cheese, shredded
2 cups flour
1 pound pitted dates
1 cup walnuts
Salt and cayenne pepper to taste

Using the steel blade of a food processor, combine butter, cheese and flour until well blended. Add dates, walnuts and seasoning; process briefly to chop dates and nuts into mixture. Remove dough from work bowl and form into long rolls, about 2 inches in diameter.

Wrap well in plastic wrap or foil and chill until firm. May be refrigerated or frozen at this point.

To bake, preheat oven to 300°. Slice dough into 1/4 inch slices and place on lightly greased cookie sheets. Bake for 20 to 30 minutes or until edges are just beginning to brown. Remove from cookie sheets and cool on wire racks. May be served hot or at room temperature. Store in air tight container.

Other Hardcovers by Great Quotations

Ancient Echoes
Behold The Golfer
Bumps in the Road
Chosen Words
Good Lies for Ladies
Great Quotes from
    Great Teachers
Great Women
Just Between Friends
Love Streams

The Essence of Music
The Perfect Brew
The Power of Inspiration
There's No Place Like
    Home
To A Very Special
    Husband
Woman to Woman
Works of Heart

Other Titles by Great Quotations

365 Reasons to Eat
    Chocolate
A Smile Increases Your
    Face Value
Aged To Perfection
Apple A Day
Champion Quotes
Close to Home
Don't Deliberate . . .
    Litigate
Each Day A New
    Beginning
For Mother–A Bouquet of
    Sentiments
Golf Humor
Good Living
I Think My Teacher
    Sleeps At School
Inspirations
Interior Design for Idiots

Money For Nothing
    Tips for Free
Mrs. Murphy's Laws
Mrs. Webster's
    Dictionary
Parenting 101
Quick Tips for Home
    Improvement
Quotes From Great
    Women
Real Estate Agents and
    Their Dirty Little Tricks
Teachers Are First Class
The Dog Ate My Car
    Keys
The Secret Language
    of Men
The Secret Language of
    Women
Thinking of You
What To Tell Children

GREAT QUOTATIONS PUBLISHING
1967 Quincy Court
Glendale Heights, IL 60139-2045
Phone (708) 582-2800, Fax (708) 582-2813